CANADA GOLD

Mario Lemieux of Montreal pumps his fist after a review of the play gave Canada a goal to tie the game against the Czech Republic during the second period of their Salt Lake City Winter Olympic hockey match, Monday, February 18, 2002 in Kearns, Utah. The game ended in a 3–3 tie. (AP Photo/Kevork Djansezian)

The Canadian Press

CANADA GOLD

CANADIAN MEN & WOMEN HOCKEY CHAMPIONS

FOREWORD BY HAYLEY WICKENHEISER

EDITED BY STEVEN PROCTOR

WINDING
STAIR
PRESS

CANADA GOLD
© 2002 by Winding Stair Press

National Library of Canada Cataloguing in Publication Data Available
ISBN 1-55366-087-0

Winding Stair Press
An imprint of Stewart House Publishing Inc.
290 North Queen Street, #210
Etobicoke, Ontario, M9C 5K4
Canada
1-866-574-6873
www.stewarthouse.com

Executive Vice President and Publisher: Ken Proctor
Director of Publishing and Product Acquisition: Joe March
Production Manager: Ruth Bradley-St-Cyr
Cover design: Darrin Laframboise (Stewart House) and Sean Vokey (CP)
Interior: Brady Typesetting and Design
Photo Editor: Mike Harvey

This book is available at special discounts for bulk purchases by groups or
organizations for sales promotions, premiums, fundraising and educational
purposes. For details, contact: Peter March, Stewart House Publishing Inc.,
Special Sales Department, 195 Allstate Parkway, Markham, Ontario L3R 4T8.
Toll free 1-866-474-3478.

1 2 3 4 5 6   07 06 05 04 03 02

Printed and bound in Canada.

To the Canadian men's & women's Olympic hockey teams

Olympic gold medallist Hayley Wickenheiser, of Shaunavon, Sask., kisses her son Noah Pachina following Canada's 3-2 victory against USA in women's hockey tournament at the Olympic Winter Games in Salt Lake City, Utah, Thursday February 21, 2002. (CP PHOTO/Tom Hanson)

February 21st, 2002 will be remembered as the date Canada's women's hockey team made history at the Salt Lake City Olympics.

We had to work hard and overcome adversity to get into the final game against the USA. No one thought we would win, but we came together like no other team I've played on, and, against all odds, we won the gold medal.

As the last five seconds of the game ticked down, everything was a blur. My final thoughts were to keep the puck on the outside of the ice and then find Kim St-Pierre, our goalie, and jump on her!

I have never been so proud to be Canadian! To stand there with my son Noah in my arms, the gold medal around my shoulders and the Canadian anthem playing was amazing. It was the fulfilment of all my childhood dreams growing up in a farming town called Shaunavon, Saskatchewan.

Little did we know that the Canadian men would make more history just three days later. With the expectations of a nation riding on their shoulders, they downed the U.S. 5-2 to secure the first men's hockey gold in 50 years and the first double gold ever by men's and women's hockey teams from the same country.

Under the leadership of the great Wayne Gretzky, they rebounded from a slow start, shrugged off intense criticism and brought the gold back to where it belongs! Our team had the pleasure of attending the game, and I will never forget how the Canadian fans sang "O Canada" with about 30 seconds remaining on the clock.

I wasn't born when Canada defeated Russia in the 1972 Summit series, but it has been the touchstone of Canadian hockey glory for me and for a generation of Canadians. I hope our double gold performance will inspire future generations the way I was inspired by the 1972 series.

There is nothing that brings people in Canada together like hockey! It is our passion. We live and breath it and we expect to be the best. Now, we are the best—at least for the next four years. But we must not get complacent. The world has caught up to Canada and while they may be able to match our skill and speed, we have something no other country has: unbeatable pride and passion for the best game in the world!

Let's use our double gold as a way to inspire our children and improve our game so we can continue to be the best for many years to come!

Hayley Wickenheiser

HAYLEY WICKENHEISER

Contents

Wayne Gretzky's fingerprints all over Canadian men's Olympic team

January 28, 2002

By PIERRE LEBRUN
The Canadian Press

Wayne Gretzky had a finger on every detail in assembling the 23-man Canadian men's Olympic hockey team.

Philadelphia Flyers' Keith Primeau (right) and New York Rangers' Eric Lindros (left) take a breather during practice at the Canadian Olympic hockey camp in Calgary Tuesday September 4, 2001.
(CP PHOTO/ Adrian Wyld)

Win or lose come Salt Lake City, this is The Great One's team.

Bob Nicholson, the president of the Canadian Hockey Association, took somewhat of a gamble on naming Gretzky executive director of the Olympic team, given Gretzky's lack of experience on the general managing side of hockey matters.

But Gretzky was busy from the start. He hinted that it was a must for young Olympic hopefuls to play for Canada at the world hockey championships in Hannover, Germany last May and they were there, playing under Gretzky's watchful eyes.

Ryan Smyth, Eric Brewer and Mike Peca played well for Canada at the world championships and were rewarded with a berth on the Olympic team.

Wade Redden and Derek Morris also went to Hannover and at least got invited to the summer orientation camp.

Jason Allison, the NHL's fourth-best scorer last season, skipped on Germany and Gretzky skipped on him.

Even the little things mattered to Gretzky. He gave his input on the design and look of Team Canada's sweaters for the 2002 Games.

Gretzky insisted on having a summer training camp and got it after a drawn-out battle with the NHL Players' Association and the International Ice Hockey Federation.

And when he was given permission only for a 48-hour camp, he privately pushed for more.

Through his captain, Mario Lemieux, that was taken care of the first night when the players arrived in Calgary. They got on the ice and practised four straight days in defiance of their own union.

"If the European teams and the NHLPA are mad, they can be mad at me — that's fine," said Gretzky.

Gretzky wanted a team that blended youth and experience with the emphasis on speed and skill — especially on defence.

Say hello to Brewer and Ed Jovanovski, a pair of young blue-liners who skate like the wind. Gretzky said goodbye to gritty veteran Scott Stevens, a player whose game didn't fit the mould of this Team Canada.

Gretzky passed over the NHL's all-time winningest coach in Scotty Bowman and picked Pat Quinn for his head coach because he thought Quinn would share his vision of a quick-transition team.

It was Gretzky who made the decision not to name a goalie among the first eight players announced last March.

That meant Patrick Roy, the NHL leader in all-time wins, would have to fight like the rest of the Canadian hopefuls.

Whether or not Roy's pride was hurt and led to his stunning announcement that he wouldn't play for Canada isn't known.

But what is clear is that Curtis Joseph is now the number one contender for the starting job in Salt Lake, the same Joseph whose "check your ego at the door" mantra endeared him to Gretzky.

The team comes first and there are no exceptions with Gretzky.

Surrounded by an impressive cast of hockey minds such as Quinn, Ken Hitchcock, Jacques Martin, Wayne Fleming, Kevin Lowe and Steve Tambellini, Gretzky was the most vocal and dominating in the behind-the-scenes meetings.

He had ideas and opinions and stated them without hesitation.

Team Canada executive director Wayne Gretzky signs autographs for fans following the second day of the Team Canada hockey orientation camp in Calgary, Wednesday, September 5, 2001. An eight-foot high fence has been erected to keep autograph-seeking fans from hounding the all-star lineup of hockey players.
(Calgary Sun/Jim Wells)

In a Toronto hotel room, on the eve of Canada's December 15 announcement of the final roster, Gretzky pretty much got the team he wanted with little opposition.

Wayne Gretzky, the hockey executive, appears headed for more greatness.

Men's Team Roster

NO.	NAME	L/R	HEIGHT (cm)	WEIGHT (kg)
2	MACINNIS, Al	R	188	95
3	BREWER, Eric	L	190	100
4	BLAKE, Rob	R	190	98
9	KARIYA, Paul	L	178	82
11	NOLAN, Owen	R	185	95
12	IGINLA, Jarome	L	185	92
14	SHANAHAN, Brendan	L	191	91
19	YZERMAN, Steve	R	180	82
20	BELFOUR, Ed	L	180	88
21	GAGNÉ, Simon	L	183	84
25	NIEUWENDYK, Joe	L	185	93
27	NIEDERMAYER, Scott	L	185	90
30	BRODEUR, Martin	L	188	93
31	JOSEPH, Curtis	L	180	86
37	PECA, Mike	R	180	86
44	PRONGER, Chris	L	198	100
52	FOOTE, Adam	R	185	93
55	JOVANOVSKI, Ed	L	188	95
66	LEMIEUX, Mario	R	193	102
74	FLEURY, Theo	R	167	81
88	LINDROS, Eric	R	193	107
91	SAKIC, Joe	L	180	86
94	SMYTH, Ryan	L	185	88

POSITION	DATE OF BIRTH	REGULAR TEAM
D	11/07/63	St. Louis Blues
D	17/04/79	Edmonton Oilers
D	10/12/69	Colorado Avalanche
F	16/10/74	Mighty Ducks of Anaheim
F	12/02/72	San Jose Sharks
F	01/07/77	Calgary Flames
F	23/01/69	Detroit Red Wings
F	09/05/65	Detroit Red Wings
G	21/04/65	Dallas Stars
F	29/02/80	Philadelphia Flyers
F	10/09/66	Dallas Stars
D	31/08/73	New Jersey Devils
G	06/05/72	New Jersey Devils
G	29/04/67	Toronto Maple Leafs
F	26/03/74	New York Islanders
D	10/10/74	St. Louis Blues
D	10/07/71	Colorado Avalanche
D	26/06/76	Vancouver Canucks
F	05/10/65	Pittsburgh Penguins
F	29/06/68	New York Rangers
F	28/02/73	New York Rangers
F	07/07/69	Colorado Avalanche
F	21/02/76	Edmonton Oilers

Canada deemed the underdog in the women's Olympic hockey tournament

February 4, 2002

By NEIL STEVENS
The Canadian Press

The Canadian women's hockey team wasn't able to beat the United States in eight meetings this season, and then there was the turmoil swirling around the late release of Nancy Drolet.

Well, let's just throw in the towel.

Give up.

Quit.

No, too much time and effort have been poured into this project for the veteran-laden lineup captained by Cassie Campbell to go to Salt Lake City with anything less than total commitment to win gold.

That's exactly how the players feel now.

"We're really looking forward to getting there," says coach Daniele Sauvageau. "It seems as if we have been preparing forever.

"We just want to go."

Sauvageau cut Drolet on January 14 and replaced her with 20-year-old Cherie Piper of Toronto. Drolet, 28, appealed the decision to the Canadian Hockey Association, but a three-member panel voted unanimously Friday to reject Drolet's plea.

Drolet is the third-leading goal scorer in Canadian women's national team history, and her overtime goals in 1997 and 2000 won Canada world championships. She was also on the Canadian team that won silver when women's hockey made its Olympic debut in 1998 in Nagano.

But Sauvageau wasn't happy with Drolet's offensive production this season — six goals and four assists in 17 games.

It's not the first time that controversy has emerged from the women's

Canada's Hayley Wickenheiser, of Shaunavon, Saskatchewan, skates past US and Canadian fans during the warm-up prior to the gold medal women's hockey game. (CP PHOTO/ Paul Chiasson)

team as it headed into the Olympics. Prior to the 1998 Games, then-coach Shannon Miller cut veteran Angela James from the Olympic roster and James complained that she had been treated unfairly.

A Canadian Hockey investigation ruled in Miller's favour, but not before rumours came to light that there had been a romance between a staff member and another player. Officials ruled that those allegations had no merit.

Despite its inability to beat the Americans this season, Sauvageau says "the excitement level is high" on the club.

"The players have been working very, very hard," she said. "They are very committed.

"There's a lot of smiles on the faces now."

Canada went 35-0 in winning seven consecutive women's world championships, but will be the underdog in the Olympic tournament.

How's that?

The Americans geared up to win the inaugural Olympic tournament in 1998, and they again appear to have timed things perfectly.

Coach Ben Smith's team, the runner-up in all those world tournaments, is 31-0-0 this season, including 8-0-0 against Canada. Yet it's a streak he's trying to downplay.

"The truth is, the difference is not that much," he says of the two powerhouses of women's hockey. "Salt Lake City will be the place where the rubber hits the road."

Canada is 11-8-0 this season, and some of its games against the Americans could have gone either way.

Members of the Canadian women's hockey team from left, Lori Dupuis (12), France St. Louis (3), and Karen Nystrom (89) react following their loss to the U.S. in their finals match at the XVIII Winter Olympics in Nagano, Japan, Tuesday, February 17, 1998. USA won 3-1 to take the gold, and Canada took silver. (AP Photo/ Hans Deryk)

"We firmly believe we've played better and better against them, although we haven't got the results on the scoreboard," says Sauvageau.

The Olympic final is scheduled for February 21. Given the weakness of the other entries, another Canada-U.S. showdown is a fait accompli.

Campbell and assistant captains Hayley Wickenheiser and Vicky Sunohara are Canada's leaders.

"We're privileged to have leadership like this," says Sauvageau.

Wickenheiser summed up her feelings and those of her teammates after losing an eighth straight to the Americans in January.

"I've never lost eight games in a row in my entire hockey career," she said. "This is tough but it's going to make Salt Lake City that much better.

"We have a lot to prove and we have nothing to lose now."

Sami Jo Small and Kim St-Pierre provide excellent goaltending. Their teammates are comfortable with either in the nets. The coaching staff hasn't announced who will play the first game in Salt Lake City.

In round-robin play at Nagano, Canada beat Sweden 5-3, lost 7-4 to the Americans, defeated Japan 13-0, blanked China 2-0, and edged Finland 4-2. The format called for the top two teams to face off for the gold medal, and the U.S. defeated Canada 3-1 in the final. Finland defeated China 4-1 to win bronze.

Germany and Kazakhstan have been added this time, and a pool format will be introduced. Canada opens against Kazakhstan on February 11.

Sauvageau has made adjustments that she says will put her players on more of an even footing with the Americans by then.

"It's a short tournament where anything can happen," she says. "We're going to Salt Lake City with confidence.

"We're going to stay focused on gold. That is what we want to achieve."

Despite being winless against the Americans, nothing has been decided yet.

"That's why we drop the puck," says Sauvageau.

Women's Team Roster

NO.	NAME	L/R	HEIGHT (ft/in)	WEIGHT (lbs)
32	LABONTÉ, Charline	L	5'08	170
1	SMALL, Sami Jo	L	5'07	187
33	ST-PIERRE, Kim	L	5'08	155
6	BRISSON, Thérèse	R	5'07	150
73	CHARTRAND, Isabelle	L	5'05	135
91	HEANEY, Geraldine	R	5'08	140
4	KELLAR, Becky	L	5'07	150
11	POUNDER, Cheryl	R	5'06	145
5	SOSTORICS, Colleen	R	5'04	170
23	ANTAL, Dana	R	5'07	135
24	BÉCHARD, Kelly	R	5'09	145
17	BOTTERILL, Jennifer	L	5'09	160
77	CAMPBELL, Cassie	L	5'08	141
7	PIPER, Cherie	R	5'05	165
12	DUPUIS, Lori	L	5'08	165
15	GOYETTE, Danielle	L	5'07	148
18	HEFFORD, Jayna	R	5'05	140
13	OUELLETTE, Caroline	L	5'11	172
25	SHEWCHUK, Tammy Lee	R	5'04	130
61	SUNOHARA, Vicky	L	5'07	170
22	WICKENHEISER, Hayley	R	5'09	170

POSITION	DATE OF BIRTH	HOMETOWN	REGULAR TEAM
G	10/15/82	Boisbriand, QC	Mistral de Laval, QC
G	03/25/76	Winnipeg, MB	Brampton Thunder, ON
G	12/14/78	Châteauguay, QC	McGill Univ. (CIAU)
D	10/05/66	Dollard des Ormeaux, QC	Mississauga Ice Bears, ON
D	04/20/78	Anjou, QC	St. Lawrence Univ. (ECAC)
D	10/01/67	Weston, ON	Beatrice Aeros, ON
D	01/01/75	Hagersville, ON	Beatrice Aeros, ON
D	06/21/76	Mississauga, ON	Beatrice Aeros, ON
D	12/17/79	Kennedy, SK	Oval X-Treme, AB
F	04/19/77	Esterhazy, SK	Oval X-Treme, AB
F	01/22/78	Sedley, SK	Oval X-Treme, AB
F	05/01/79	Winnipeg, MB	Harvard Univ. (ECAC)
F	11/22/73	Brampton, ON	Oval X-Treme, AB
F	06/29/81	Scarborough, ON	Beatrice Aeros, ON
F	11/14/72	Cornwall, ON	Brampton Thunder, ON
F	01/30/66	St-Nazaire, QC	Oval X-Treme, AB
F	05/14/77	Kingston, ON	Brampton Thunder, ON
F	05/25/79	Montréal, QC	Wingstar de Montréal, QC
F	12/31/77	St-Laurent, QC	Harvard Univ. (ECAC)
F	05/18/70	Scarborough, ON	Brampton Thunder, ON
F	08/12/78	Shaunavon, SK	Oval X-Treme, AB

Exhausted Kazakh goaltender Natalya Trunova, wearing a satisfied smile under a University of Oklahoma cap covered in Olympic pins that was given to her by the team bus driver, said her side "expected a difficult game with the Canadians.

"I'm very tired, but I don't think that had anything to do with my performance," she added.

After Wickenheiser scored the first of five Canadian power-play goals 2:33 into the game, Piper banged the rebound of a shot by linemate Dana Antal of Esterhazy, Saskatchewan, past Trunova at 8:45.

The rebound of Piper's shot from the slot was put in by Sunohara on a power play at 11:09.

"It's actually a relief that I stepped in and made some plays, but it doesn't matter who scores as long as the team wins," said Piper, who added that playing in the Olympics is "no longer a dream.

(Previous page) *Canada's coach Daniele Sauvageau, center, directs her players Jayna Hefford, right, and Lori Dupuis in the third period against Kazakhstan.* (AP Photo/ Kevork Djansezian)

Canada's Kelly Bechard (24) attempts to knock the puck loose from Kazakhstan goalkeeper Natalya Trunova's glove during the third period. (AP Photo/ Kevork Djansezian)

"The dream's over and now we have to perform."

Drolet was the third-leading scorer in team history with 112 points in 108 international games, but team management was concerned that her play had dropped off after she was named to the Olympic squad in November.

They also felt their second-line centre was not producing enough against the United States, the defending Olympic champions who are the only real rivals to Canada for the gold medal.

And, while they don't say it, the team sent a message that veterans can no longer be complacent about their positions, especially after it lost all eight pre-Olympic games with the U.S. this season.

A shocked Drolet took her case to a Sport Canada appeals panel, but was turned down.

"We made a change and we decided to pick Cherie for many reasons," said head coach Daniele Sauvageau of Montreal. "Cherie doesn't replace Nancy Drolet.

"She was at all our practices and played a lot of games for us this year. She's been part of the team since Day One. And I'm very happy with how she played. She can play centre or wing and she's a tough cookie to play against."

After being left off the original roster, Piper stayed on as an alternate, waiting to step in if there was an injury. Instead, Drolet was cut.

"I was with the team, so it's not like I was out of the picture and then back in it," said Piper, a declared Boston fan who counts rugged former Bruins' star Cam Neely as her favourite hockey player.

"But it didn't sink in until I phoned my friends and family to tell them I'm going (to the Olympics). It's great that the team had faith in me and that my teammates welcomed me back."

Canada has a much tougher test on Wednesday against a rapidly improving Russia and closes out the opening round on Saturday against Sweden.

Canada's Vicky Sunohara celebrates her goal against Kazakhstan goalkeeper Natalya Trunova during the first period.
(AP Photo/Kevork Djansezian)

Kazakhstan has a relatively new program and its smaller, slower and less experienced players were hard-pressed to keep up with seven-time world champion Canada.

Kazakhstan's best chance came late in the second period when veteran Thérèse Brisson of Montreal turned over the puck at the blue-line and Natalya Yakovchuk went in on a breakaway, but failed to beat goaltender Kim St-Pierre of Montreal from in close.

It was actually an improved performance for Kazakhstan, which lost 11-0 to Canada and was outshot 63-6 at the world championships last spring.

Coach Alexander Maltsev said playing against Canada let the Kazakhs "see our progress and what needs to be done.

"To lose to Canada is an honour."

Canada vs. Kasakhstan Game Summary

FIRST PERIOD	1. Canada, Wickenheiser 2:33 (pp)
	2. Canada, Piper (Antal, Sostorics) 8:45
	3. Canada, Sunohara (Piper, Ouellette) 11:09 (pp)
PENALTIES	Taikevich Kaz (holding) 2:30
	Botterill Cda (high-sticking) 3:51
	Khlyzova Kaz (slashing) 9:20
	Campbell Cda (tripping) 19:25
SECOND PERIOD	4. Canada, Shewchuk (Goyette, Sostorics) 3:49 (pp)
	5. Canada, Wickenheiser (Goyette) 15:18 (pp)
PENALTIES	Brisson Cda (boarding) 1:37
	Taikevich Kaz (slashing) 3:04
	Taikevich Kaz (high-sticking) 5:10
	Taikevich Kaz (tripping) 9:14
	Kazakhstan bench (delay of game; served by Alexeyeva) 14:16
	Shtelmaister Kaz (holding) 17:02
	Potapova Kaz (tripping) 20:00
THIRD PERIOD	6. Canada, Goyette (Wickenheiser) 7:27 (pp)
	7. Canada, Sunohara (Hefford) 17:29
PENALTIES	Solovyeva Kaz (holding) 6:57
	Ouellette Cda (roughing) 8:28
SHOTS ON GOAL	Kazakhstan 3 3 5—11
	Canada 24 18 24—66
GOAL	Kazakhstan: Natalya Trunova
	Canada: Kim St-Pierre
POWER-PLAYS *(goals-chances)*	Kazakhstan: 0-4
	Canada: 5-9

February 13, 2002

SALT LAKE CITY (CP) — Hayley Wickenheiser and the Canadian women's hockey team continue to roll at the Winter Games.

Wickenheiser had a goal and two assists to lead Canada to a lopsided 7-0 victory over Russia on Wednesday. It marked the second straight game that the Canadians had dominated their opposition.

On Monday, Canada dispatched Kazakhstan by an identical 7-0 verdict.

Russia's Olga Savenkova, left, high sticks Canada's Hayley Wickenheiser of Shaunavon, Saskatchewan during the second period. Wickenheiser had a goal and two assists to lead Canada to a 7–0 victory over Russia. (AP Photo/ Kevork Djansezian)

"I don't think that in talent and conditioning we're that much behind (Canada)," said Russia's Ekaterina Pachkevich, who is on a leave of absence from a coaching job at MIT in Boston and speaks fluent English. "The difference is choosing from 200 players in Russia and 50,000 in Canada."

By virtue of Wednesday's win, Canada (2-0) qualified for the medal round, which begins Tuesday. The Canadians will play their final round-robin game. By downing Russia, Canada clinched a berth in the medal round that begins Tuesday.

The Canadians will conclude round-robin play Saturday against Sweden.

As she did against Kazakhstan, Wickenheiser opened the scoring against Russia before setting up two goals by linemate Danielle Goyette.

Dana Antal, Cherie Piper, Jennifer Botterill and Isabelle Chartrand had the other goals for Canada.

Canada's Danielle Goyette of St-Nazaire, Québec, gets squeezed out of the play by Russia's Svetlana Trefilova (left) and Zhanna Shchelchkova during the second period.
(COA/Mike Ridewood)

Canada outshot Russia 60-6. In their two games, the Canadians have outshot their opposition by a whopping 126-17 margin.

Canada vs. Russia Game Summary

FIRST PERIOD	1. Canada, Wickenheiser 11:37
	2. Canada, Goyette (Wickenheiser) 18:00
PENALTIES	Botterill Cda (high-sticking) 5:44
SECOND PERIOD	3. Canada, Antal (Ouellette, Heaney) 0:31
	4. Canada, Piper (Ouellette, Botterill) 9:14
PENALTIES	Tsareva Rus (checking from behind) 7:03
	Antal Cda (high-sticking) 10:00
	Tretyakova Rus (hooking) 13:24
THIRD PERIOD	5. Canada, Botterill (Sunohara, Brisson) 7:48 (pp)
	6. Canada, Chartrand 18:12
	7. Canada, Goyette (Wickenheiser) 18:50
PENALTIES	Smolentseva Rus (roughing) 5:52
	Smolentseva Rus (body-checking) 15:23
SHOTS ON GOAL	Canada 14 19 27–60
	Russia 1 3 2–6
GOAL	Canada: Sami Jo Small
	Russia: Irina Gashennikova
POWER-PLAYS *(goals-chances)*	Canada: 1–4
	Russia: 0–2

Super Mario says entire year dedicated to helping Canada win gold medal

February 13, 2002

By PIERRE LEBRUN

SALT LAKE CITY (CP) — A fired-up Mario Lemieux descended upon the Winter Games in Salt Lake City on Wednesday and made no bones about his plans to bring back Canada's first gold medal in men's hockey in 50 years.

"My priority this year was to play in the Olympics and that's why I haven't played too many (NHL) games, especially in the last couple of weeks," said the Canadian team captain to over 150 journalists on Wednesday night.

"I'm really looking forward to it, to have a chance to play with these great players and to give everything I have over the next 10 days. To bring back the gold medal to Canada would be something very special."

Lemieux was careful in his preparation, avoiding any back-to-back games since his return from hip surgery last month.

"I've been thinking about the Olympics for a while and that's why I skipped a few games prior to the Olympics just to make sure that I would get to the Olympics," said the Pittsburgh Penguins' centre.

Lemieux was asked about the pressure Team Canada was under to deliver after the fourth-place finish four years ago in Nagano, Japan. He didn't hesitate in his answer.

"I've welcomed to play under pressure and it seems to bring the best out of me," said Lemieux, who was retired in 1998 and not on Canada's team. "It's something that I enjoy. I don't shy away from it. We all know the pressure we have here in the next 10 days.

"If you're not able to play under pressure, maybe you should be watching it on TV. We're all professionals here, we all know what's at stake, we all have a lot of confidence in each other and I think it's going to show over the next 10 days."

Lemieux hasn't arrived at Salt Lake alone. He decided to bring along his family, including five-year-old son Austin, for support in a pressure-cooker situation.

"Austin's a big hockey fan and loves to play the game. It's going to be a great 10 days for him," Lemieux said.

"We know it's going to be very emotional in the next 10 days and through tough times it's always good to have your family around you for support and that's one of the reasons I decided to bring the whole family."

Winning a gold medal would cap off a remarkable career for Lemieux, who also won a pair of Stanley Cups with the Pens in 1990–91 and 1991–92.

"It's a difficult question," he said in French when asked about comparing the Olympic gold to a Stanley Cup. "The Stanley Cups I won in Pittsburgh are something really special. You grow up dreaming about winning it as a kid.

"But there's no doubt a gold medal would be just as special."

Lemieux hits the ice for Canada's first practice Thursday at 5 p.m. EST.

Most of the team arrives Thursday and will head straight to the practice arena.

Meanwhile, it does not appear likely that Boston Bruins centre Joe Thornton will be added to Canada's team. Centre Steve Yzerman, who underwent minor knee surgery two weeks ago, has played a pair of games with the Detroit Red Wings and appears fully fit.

Wingers Paul Kariya (finger) and Owen Nolan (back) and defenceman Al MacInnis (ankle) are also set to go meaning the 23-man roster chosen on December 15 will remain intact heading into Friday's opening game against Sweden.

"As of this morning, we have a green light on all of our players," said Team Canada head coach Pat Quinn, also present at the news conference that lasted about half an hour. "A couple of the ones who were question marks, or wait-and-see situations, have played and have played successfully and played again tonight in two cases.

"I would say that as of Thursday at 3 p.m. we do not foresee having to make any changes because of injuries."

Quinn was asked about the dreaded shootout, certainly not the last time that will happen in the next week considering the Canadians were knocked about by the Czech Republic in semi-final shootout four years ago.

"We'll be prepared for it," Quinn said. "And I'm approaching it like we're going to get it done this time.

"But my first aim is not even to get there," he added. "I want to win it straight up, 60-minute regulation time, Sunday afternoon (February 24). I've already seen it."

Sweden sinks Canada 5-2

February 15, 2002

By BILL BEACON

West Valley, Utah (CP)— The Swedish torpedo exploded for four second-period goals as Sweden overwhelmed Canada 5-2 in their opening hockey game at the 2002 Winter Olympics on Friday night.

Toronto Maple Leafs captain Mats Sundin had two goals and an assist to lead Sweden, which entered the Olympics as underdogs without their star – injured centre Peter Forsberg.

"It was embarrassing," Team Canada forward Paul Kariya said after the game.

(Opposite)
Canada forward Mario Lemieux (66), of Montreal, sends Sweden forward Daniel Alfredsson sprawling during the second period. (CP PHOTO/ Tom Hanson)

Sweden goalie Tommy Salo stops Canada's Mario Lemieux from close range during a 5-2 Swedish win. (COA/Mike Ridewood)

Sweden forward Mats Sundin raises his arms to celebrate his goal during the first period. (CP PHOTO/ Tom Hanson)

"We've got to take this as a lesson," added Canadian coach Pat Quinn. "We got hammered. If we think we can play that way, we'll be going home Thursday morning."

Niklas Sundstrom, Kenny Jonsson and Ulf Dahlen also scored for Sweden, which used its trademark torpedo, a system of heavy forechecking, to rattle the Canadian defence.

Rob Blake scored for Canada 2:37 into the game, but after the Canadians dominated the opening five minutes, the Swedes took over with thorough checking in the neutral zone and opportunistic counterattacks.

Edmonton defenceman Eric Brewer, who struggled for most of the

game, revived Canadian hopes when he rushed past Fredrik Olausson and scored at 15:39 of the third period.

A goal by Eric Lindros 25 seconds later was disallowed because Michael Peca was in the crease – an international rule that was dropped by the NHL two years ago.

By then, the game was lost.

Once Sundin tied the game on a breakaway at 5:30 of the first frame, goaltender Curtis Joseph fought the puck and failed to make the big saves Canada needed to stay in the game.

Martin Brodeur is expected to be in goal when Canada tries to rebuild its shaken confidence in its second round robin game on Sunday against Germany.

"There's two more games before the real tournament starts," said

Theoren Fleury (14) of Canada is kept off the scoreboard by Sweden's goalie Tommy Salo and defenceman Mattias Nordstrom.
(CP PHOTO/HO/COA/ Mike Ridewood)

Team Canada captain Mario Lemieux, who was scoreless with one shot in his Olympic debut. "We still have time to get it together."

No teams are eliminated from the round robin, which only determines seedings for the quarter-finals next week.

"I wouldn't read much into this," Canada forward Theo Fleury said. "It's great for us, actually, because it makes us an underdog, and that's what we like."

The nearly full E-Centre, which seats just over 8,000, was a sea of flags with the Maple Leaf outnumbering the Swedish Tre Kroner four to one.

But Canadian fans had little reason to wave them.

The Canadians were a step behind the Swedes on the wider Olympic ice surface and looked confused and tentative with the new international rule eliminating the red-line for off-sides.

Ottawa captain Daniel Alfredsson used a clever two-line pass to send

Canada goaltender Curtis Joseph, of Toronto, sprawls in front of the goal as Sweden forward Jorgen Jonsson (42) celebrates his brother Kenny's goal during the second period.
(CP PHOTO/ Tom Hanson)

Sundin in on his breakaway. Sundin beat his Leafs teamate Joseph cleanly between the pads.

Sundstrom got away from Steve Yzerman's checking to work the puck in front and lift a shot over the sprawled Joseph 6:06 into the second frame to begin the Swedish barrage.

As Canadian team boss Wayne Gretzky and general manager Kevin Lowe looked on glumly from the grandstands, Sundin scored on a blast from the left circle at 10:42.

Defenceman Chris Pronger was caught pinching as Jonsson finished a two-on-one with Swedish league player Henrik Zetterberg at 11:47. Pronger was caught again as Dahlen slipped behind him to score on a power play at 15:58.

Canada had two of its three power play opportunities in the final period and, on its best chance, Lemieux had the puck checked off his stick by Jonsson with the net gaping open.

On another chance, Tommy Salo slid out his glove to stop Fleury's spin-around shot at the edge of the crease.

Scott Niedermayer drilled a slapshot off the crossbar in the second period and Joe Nieuwendyk lifted one off the bar in the first.

Canada vs. Sweden Game Summary

SWEDEN 5, CANADA 2

FIRST PERIOD	1. Canada, Blake (Peca, Fleury) 2:37
	2. Sweden, Sundin (Alfredsson) 5:30
PENALTY	Sundin Swe (holding) 11:31
SECOND PERIOD	3. Sweden, Sundstrom (Nylander, Naslund) 6:06
	4. Sweden, Sundin (Alfredsson, Lidstrom) 10:42
	5. Sweden, K. Jonsson (Zetterberg) 11:47
	6. Sweden, Dahlen (Sundstrom, Sundin) 15:58 (pp)
PENALTY	MacInnis Cda (high-sticking) 15:18
THIRD PERIOD	7. Canada, Brewer (Nolan) 15:39
PENALTIES	Olausson Swe (delay of game) 0:27
	Ragnarsson Swe (tripping) 7:16
SHOTS ON GOAL	Sweden 10 11 4-25
	Canada 15 3 17-35
GOAL	Sweden: Tommy Salo
	Canada: Curtis Joseph
POWER-PLAYS *(goals-chances)*	Sweden: 1-1
	Canada: 0-3

(opposite page)
Tammy Lee Shewchuk of Canada celebrates in front team Sweden members Annica Ahlen (35) and Gunilla Andersson (23).
(AP Photo/ Lawrence Jackson)

Twenty cheerleaders positioned at the base of the stands helped keep the decibel level high.

Botterill opened the scoring at 10:26. She took a pass from Tammy Lee Shewchuk at Sweden's blue-line, stickhandled around Gunilla Andersson on the right wing for a clear path to the net, cut across the front of the crease, and reached to plant the puck into the far side of the net before goalie Annica Ahlen could shift across to cover.

It would be Canada's only goal on 19 shots but Ahlen's armour melted in the second period.

Piper batted in a bouncing puck, and Botterill got her second of the game when she raised her stick to deflect in a long shot by Geraldine Heaney on a power play.

Wickhenheiser, set up by a pass from Cassie Campbell, beat Ahlen

Lori Dupuis (12) of Canada battles with Nanna Jansson of Sweden in the first period. (AP Photo/ Lawrence Jackson)

that broke open a tight, defensive contest.

"We have a lot of guys who haven't played together, but it's starting to come. I just think we need a few more days."

After a nervous first period marked by misfired shots and a botched breakaway by Michael Peca, it was Joe Sakic who broke the ice when he slid the puck under goaltender Marc Seliger at 8:59 of the second frame.

Kariya and Adam Foote added goals, but Canada nearly got burned while trying to sit on the lead in the third, when Andreas Loth and Jochen Hecht scored in a determined German comeback attempt.

Canada and the defending Olympic champion Czech Republic, both

1-1, face each other on Monday at the E-Center in West Valley City, Utah with second place in their round robin group at stake.

Sweden defeated the Czech Republic 2-1 earlier Sunday.

Head coach Pat Quinn shuffled the lines after Canada's shocking 5-2 loss to Sweden in the tournament opener Friday, when a disjointed Canadian side was run out of the rink in a disastrous second period.

The changes were partly prompted by the absence of team captain Mario Lemieux, who sat out of Sunday's game after a nagging hip injury flared up during Friday's game.

Quinn said no decision had been made yet on whether Lemieux would play against the Czechs.

Canada's Simon Gagné of Ste-Foy, Québec, looks for a rebound as German goaltender Marc Seliger makes a save during the second period. (AP Photo/ Lawrence Jackson)

Paul Kariya of North Vancouver, British Columbia, celebrates after scoring a goal against Germany in the second period. (AP Photo/ Lawrence Jackson)

Canada played a smarter game against Germany, staying closer together on the ice and rarely letting themselves get lured into trying the long, high-risk passes that are encouraged by international hockey's rule of having no red-line.

"I definitely think that once they find the harmony between themselves, they'll be OK," German winger Mark McKay, from Brandon, Manitoba, said of the Canadian team.

"They've got way too much talent out there not to contend. I think it's a matter of time for them to find their game."

Canada still had trouble putting passes together against a gritty German team that kept five skaters strung across its blue-line to break up Canadian attacks and launch counter-offences.

(Opposite) Scott *Niedermayer (27) of Cranbrook, British Columbia, keeps an eye on the puck as Daniel Kreutzer (26) of Germany checks him in the first period.* (AP Photo/ Lawrence Jackson)

Much the same German team used similar tactics to hold Canada to a 3-3 tie at the world championships last April.

The Czechs also play a defensive game, but have far more talent to capitalize on the counter-attacks

"We were a lot better through the neutral zone," said centre Peca. "It took us a period to finally find it.

"They were lined up at the blue-line. And it was big on the power play to capitalize on two."

Actually, Foote's goal came a second after a power play ended. He scored on a wrist shot from the point with Joe Nieuwendyk screening German goaltender Marc Seliger at 18:25 of the second frame.

Canada got the five-minute power play when Daniel Kunce hammered Ryan Smyth's face into the glass with a check from behind.

Team Canada's Brendan Shanahan, centre, trys a wrap around past Germany's Wayne Hynes and goaltender Marc Seliger during the first period. (Winnipeg Free Press/Joe Bryksa)

Smyth suffered two cuts over his left eye — one that needed two stitches and the other that needed seven.

With the man advantage, Kariya lifted the rebound of an Owen Nolan shot over Seliger at 13:24.

The Peaks Ice Arena, a community facility jammed with 6,425 spectators, was awash with flag-waving Canadian fans who agonized as a still unsynchronized team struggled to make plays on the wider international ice surface.

"We can't worry about what people back home are thinking," said Sakic. "We held on for 3-2, but the first two periods showed we're progressing.

"We know we're going to get better. There's not much time to find chemistry and that's why they tinkered with the line combinations. But it's not that difficult to get used to each other. With the skill level out there, guys are smart enough to learn to play with anyone."

With Canada sitting back in the final period, Loth finished a rush with McKay at 7:36 and Hecht scored on a shot that went off goaltender Martin Brodeur's shoulder and dropped into the net on a power play at 13:51.

Canada outshot the Germans 37-20, including 17-4 in the second period, in Brodeur's first-ever start in goal at an Olympics.

Canada vs. Germany Game Summary

FIRST PERIOD	No scoring
PENALTIES	Lindros Cda (roughing) 0:24
	Ehrhoff Ger (cross-checking) 7:59
	Pronger Cda (high-sticking) 13:00
SECOND PERIOD	1. Canada, Sakic (Gagne) 8:59
	2. Canada, Kariya (Nolan) 14:23 (pp)
	3. Canada, Foote (Jovanovski, Nieuwendyk) 18:25
PENALTIES	Blake Cda (tripping) 4:35
	Kunce Ger (roughing major, game misconduct) 13:24
THIRD PERIOD	4. Germany, Loth (MacKay, Ludemann) 7:36
	5. Germany, Hecht (Schubert, Abstreiter) 13:51 (pp)
PENALTIES	Lindros Cda (high-sticking) 3:19
	MacInnis Cda (tripping) 12:16
SHOTS ON GOAL	Germany 8 4 8—20
	Canada 10 17 10—37
GOAL	Germany: Marc Seliger
	Canada: Martin Brodeur
POWER-PLAYS *(goals-chances)*	Germany: 1—5
	Canada: 1—3

Canadian captain nets pair in 3-3 tie with Czechs

By BILL BEACON

West Valley City, Utah (CP) – Mario Lemieux said he feels fine and that's just one more reason for Canada's anxious fans to feel better about their Olympic hockey team.

Lemieux scored twice and Joe Nieuwendyk got the tying goal with 3:24 left in the third period as Canada tied the Czech Republic 3-3 in its best game yet at the 2002 Winter Games.

"It means a lot to everybody here," said Lemieux. "There's certainly a

Canada's Paul Kariya, of North Vancouver, looks for the puck as Czech goalie Dominik Hasek goes down to make the save during the second period.

(COA/Andre Forget)

lot of pressure out there.

"It meant a lot just to play pretty well. For the 22 guys on that bench, it's important to get comfortable for the rest of the tournament. We spent a lot of time together in the last few days and I think the team gelled."

Canada and the Czech Republic both finished the round robin portion of the tournament with 1-1-1 records, but the Czechs took second place in the group because of a better goal differential – plus-five compared to minus-2 for Canada.

Jiri Dopita put the Czechs ahead at 13:17 of the third frame before Nieuwendyk tied it on a one-timer from the slot off a perfect feed from Theoren Fleury.

If Canada plays anything like it did against the Czechs, Finland could be in trouble.

(Opposite) Canada's Paul Kariya, of North Vancouver, British Columbia, left, watches as Czech Republic goalie Dominik Hasek, right, holds the puck in his glove as he falls in his net after a shot by Mario Lemieux, of Montreal, during the second period. After review of the play Lemieux was awarded the goal. The game ended in a 3-3 tie. (AP Photo/Kevork Djansezian)

Jamie Chenciner, 9, of Montreal, cheers on Team Canada during the game against the Czech Republic. (COA/ Andre Forget)

It started with Lemieux, who sat out Sunday's 3-2 win over Germany with a nagging hip injury. He returned to the line-up and played an inspired game that the rest of Team Canada followed.

"There were no problems," Lemieux said of the hip. "I had treatments the last few days and a day off and I felt better.

"I felt great from the start. I was able to skate better because I was at centre, getting some speed, supporting the play a little more."

The Canadians came out hitting and aggressively chasing every puck, hemming the Czechs in their zone for much of the first period.

"The key was to come out with intensity and play our game," said Lemieux. "That's skating, forechecking, playing more physical and taking time and space away from their defencemen.

"That's how we have to play from now on."

It was the first Olympic meeting between the sides since the Czechs' shock shootout win in the semifinals of the 1998 Games in Nagano, Japan, and it was nasty.

In the dying seconds of the third period, defenceman Roman Hamrlik first speared Ryan Smyth under the arm, then cross-checked Fleury in the back, causing him to bounce heavily off the E-Center ice.

Fleury appeared unhurt after the game, but Team Canada executive director Wayne Gretzky was livid.

It wasn't the only moment of controversy.

At 18:49 of the second period, Lemieux tied the game 2-2 on a high shot that was gloved by goaltender Dominik Hasek, who then rolled back into the net with the puck.

Video review judge Konstantin Komissarov allowed the goal to stand because the glove, with the puck in it, clearly crossed the line and Hasek

Team Canada goalie Martin Brodeur pushes Czech Milan Hejduk away from him during the first period.
(COA/Andre Forget)

was not pushed into the net, an International Ice Hockey Federation spokesman said.

"Dominik's whole body was across the line and the puck was underneath him," said Lemieux. "I was afraid they wouldn't see the puck from above, but it was over the line."

Czech coach Josef Augusta declined to argue.

"There will be no speculation – I think it was a goal," he said.

Team Canada management made the surprise decision to start Martin Brodeur in goal for a second straight game and had the designated third goalie, Ed Belfour, as the back-up. Brodeur made a spectacular lunge and grab of Jan Hrdina's blast from the slot 2:51 into the final period and was a force with his puck-handling ability throughout the match.

And Team Canada allowed their anxious fans to exhale by finally showing the skill and dominating physical play that had made them a pre-tournament favourite.

They outshot the Czechs 36-29 and did not allow a shot on Brodeur until Martin Rucinsky's wrister 4:40 into the game.

Team Canada executive director Wayne Gretzky watches Mario Lemieux skate by as Gretzky's nine-year-old son Ty takes pictures from the bench of the Canadian men's Olympic hockey team during practice.
(CP PHOTO/ Frank Gunn)

"We're the biggest story down here and they love it when we're not doing well," he said. "Now they have two Canadian stories — figure skating and the hockey team.

"It's all a crock of bull."

The tie with the Czech Republic gave Canada new optimism as it heads into a quarter-final meeting on Wednesday against a beatable team from Finland.

The red-faced Gretzky admitted he was "hot" with anger over Czech defenceman Roman Hamrlik of the New York Islanders, who speared winger Ryan Smyth and then brusquely cross-checked Theoren Fleury in the dying seconds of the game.

Fleury crumpled to the ice after the shot and was very slow in getting up.

Gretzky called Hamrlik's actions "cowardly," and said he should be suspended for the rest of the tournament. He also accused the media of holding Canada to a double standard.

"He blatantly tried to hurt (Fleury) — he cross-checked him in the back," said Gretzky. "I don't know why I wasn't asked that question, but if it was one of my players who would have done it, that's the first question I'd be asked.

"If a Canadian did that, it would be big news. If a Czech does it, it's OK. It's all a crock of crap."

Team Canada's executive director of hockey, Wayne Gretzky, put his coat on quickly and left after Canada just beat out team Germany with a score of 3-2 during Olympic hockey play Sunday February 17, 2002. (Winnipeg Free Press/ Joe Bryksa)

February 23, 2002

By PIERRE LEBRUN

WEST VALLEY CITY, Utah (CP) — Wayne Gretzky kept his temper in check for 20 years as a player. But it took only 15 months at the helm of Canada's Olympic men's hockey team to let it loose.

Make no mistake. It was always there. But Canadian hockey fans never really got to see it until The Great One blew up last Monday night following Canada's 3-3 tie with the Czech Republic.

Asked if he had ever seen that kind of anger before from his world-famous son, Walter Gretzky replied: "Privately, yes. Not publicly, though."

It's a new side of Wayne Gretzky for many Canadians, but it's not a new Wayne Gretzky. He always had that edge but it was well-hidden.

"He's just showing his competitive side," says Kevin Lowe, assistant GM on Team Canada and a longtime friend and teammate from the old Edmonton days. "He had so much fluidity and grace on the ice that no one could really appreciate how competitive he was — or is. I think that's what he has shown more than anything."

Even in his most devastating moment as a player, which he says was losing to Montreal in the 1993 Stanley Cup final when he was trying to bring a first-ever championship to Los Angeles, he was quiet and classy as ever after the last game at the Montreal Forum.

But now he feels the expectations of an entire country, not just one NHL city.

When Gretzky was named executive director of Team Canada on

November 8, 2000, no one quite knew what that job really entailed.

Was he a mere figurehead?

Certainly not, as it turns out. From having the final say on the team jerseys to pushing hard for the players he wanted on the roster, Gretzky has made this his project and his team.

That's why he feels so much pressure to deliver a gold medal. He knows he will shoulder a large share of the blame if Canada loses to the U.S. on Sunday.

Walter Gretzky, father of Wayne Gretzky, yells encouragement from the stands at the start of the Salt Lake City Winter Olympics hockey game between Canada and Germany.
(AP Photo/Hans Deryk)

What Gretzky has found out the hard way is that wearing the Maple Leaf as a player is a whole lot easier than running the show.

"I don't know if I've enjoyed it too much," he said with a laugh Saturday, recalling the last 15 months. "When you look back and it's over, you can think about what happened and things you did great and things that went the wrong way.

"All in all, it's tough and it's tough to win."

What few people realize is that Gretzky's anger about Canadian hockey being disrespected stems from way before these Olympics. First of all, he was stung by the semi-final shootout loss to the Czechs at the 1998 Olympics and has carried that feeling into Salt Lake.

After all, who can forget the image of Gretzky sitting on the bench after that loss, looking like the world had just crashed on him.

"I remember looking down from the stands at the bench and seeing Wayne just sitting there, alone," says Walter Gretzky. "That was his last and only Olympic chance."

A second factor in Gretzky's growing frustration was going to the world hockey championships last May in Germany and watching young but talented Team Canada get knocked out in the quarter-finals by the U.S.

The next day, when he met with a few reporters at his hotel in Hannover, Gretzky had the look of a man who had just lost Game 7 of the Stanley Cup final. He was hurt by Canada's surprising loss and angered by how much the Europeans enjoyed Canada's failure. And he was also reminded of how difficult it would be for Canada to win in Salt Lake.

So when you add up everything that Gretzky already had going in his head before these Games, his outburst here was not that surprising.

"I could see it building up," Lowe says. "There was enough stuff said. I think it has a lot to do with '98. Quite frankly, there's quite an amount of angst towards the Europeans."

Canada's general manager Wayne Gretzky watches his team practice at the Olympic Winter Games in Salt Lake City, Utah, Saturday, February 23, 2002.
(CP PHOTO/Paul Chiasson)

Still, even his father was surprised to see Wayne explode like that.

"Yes. At that press conference he said a few things," said Walter Gretzky, a little pride glowing in his eyes. "He was just trying to make people realize that we're proud Canadians and we want to win."

The players appreciate their boss's antics. After all, it took the spotlight off their slow start here and put it on him.

Women hunt gold: Canadians earn spot in final with third-period comeback

February 19, 2001

By NEIL STEVENS

West Valley City, Utah (CP) – The Canadian women's hockey team was down 3-2 to Finland to start the third period but, in the players' minds, the outcome of its Olympic semi-final Tuesday was never in doubt.

"You guys would probably really laugh if you'd been in the dressing room," Therese Brisson said of the casual intermission atmosphere she

shared with her teammates. "We were totally not worried at all.

"We talked about sealing things off on defence and not giving them any uneven rushes. Finland is a good team and when you make a mistake they'll capitalize on it, so we wanted to eliminate our errors and it was just a matter of time before the puck starting going in."

Five unanswered goals paced Canada to a 7-3 victory.

Brisson and Hayley Wickenheiser scored two goals each for the winners. Jayna Hefford, Vicky Sunohara and Cassie Campbell had the others.

Canada will play either the U.S. or Sweden for the gold medal Thursday. The Americans and Swedes faced off later Tuesday.

The Americans were overwhelming favourites to advance, and Sunohara is eager for another go at them. They've dominated Canada this season with eight straight victories.

Therese Brisson, left, of Dollard-des-Ormeaux, Québec, and Saija Sirvio (6) of Finland, battle in the first period of play in front of Finnish goalie Tuula Puputti.

(AP Photo/Lawrence Jackson)

(Opposite)

Canada's Hayley Wickenheiser, left, of Shaunavon, Saskatchewan, and teammate Cassie Campbell, of Brampton, Ontario, celebrate Campbell's third period goal in front of their bench.

(AP Photo/
Rusty Kennedy)

"It just gets us more pumped up," Sunohara said of a perceived U.S. swagger. "They've beaten us eight straight times so they've got the right to say whatever they want.

"We just want to take it into the dressing room and use it to our advantage."

Canada led Finland 2-0 by the middle of the first period but trailed 3-2 at the end of the second after Tiia Reima scored twice and Katja Riipi once.

Tiny goalie Tuula Puputti, who plays collegiate hockey at Minnesota-

Duluth, was stealing the show. Canada had outshot Finland 40-13 through two periods, but was still losing.

Breakaway goals by Wickenheiser and Hefford six seconds apart early in the third touched off Canada's scoring explosion.

"It was a tough game and we were short-handed a lot," Finnish coach Jouko Lukkarila said. "We fought like hell but it wasn't enough."

Canada outshot Finland 54-18.

It was the first serious test of the tournament for Canada, which outscored opponents 25-0 in the preliminary round.

"I think it's great we had such a tough game," said Campbell. "We've had some easy ones and we know that if we played the U.S. in the final, it's going to be tough."

Daniele Sauvageau, Canada's coach, opted to start Kim St-Pierre in goal for the second straight game after alternating her with Sami Jo Small at the start of the tournament.

"There was a goal on a 2-on-1, a loose puck, and a turnover," she said in defending St-Pierre's performance. "It's a team game, and if there is a goal, someone did something they shouldn't have. But that's what hockey is about."

Sauvageau said she will decide today who will start in goal for Canada in the gold medal game.

Geraldine Heaney, the 34-year-old defenceman who will dress for Canada for the last time Thursday, likes what she's seen of this team.

"Throughout the tournament we've got better and better and I think that's really important," she said. "We're really confident right now."

Canada can defeat the United States, said the only woman in the world to have won seven gold medals in women's world championships.

"For sure," she said. "Our team is good enough to win gold. We came here for a gold medal and nothing else. It comes down to one game and anything can happen."

Finland's Katja Riipi, left, scores her second goal of the game against Canada's goalie Kim St-Pierre, of Chateauguay, Québec, during the second period. (AP Photo/ Kevork Djansezian)

Canada erases Nagano setback with gritty 3–2 win over U.S.

February 21, 2002

By NEIL STEVENS

West Valley City, Utah (CP) – Cassie Campbell stood wrapped in a Canadian flag to receive her gold Olympic hockey medal, and she began to weep even before the ribbon holding the precious prize was dropped over her head.

Olympic gold medallists (left to right) Canada's Tammy Lee Shewchuk, of Saint-Laurent, Québec, Jennifer Botterill, of Winnipeg, Colleen Sostorics, of Kennedy, Saskatchewan, and Isabelle Chartrand, of Anju, Québec, do a victory lap with the Canadian flag.
(CP PHOTO/
Tom Hanson)

*Hayley W
heiser of Sha
Saskatchew*
*Canada's
goal thro
legs of F
goalie
Puputti, du
first per*

Tom

Canadian women's hockey team goalie Kim St-Pierre, of Chateauguay, Québec, shows her gold medal to friends and family through the glass.
(COA/Mike Ridewood)

The tears washed away the disappointment that had lingered since the previous Winter Games final.

"It's unbelievable, unbelievable," she said afterwards. "I'm afraid I'll wake up and this will have been a dream and we'll have to play the gold-medal game over again."

No worries there. The glory belongs to Canada's captain and her teammates forever.

A stunning 3-2 upset of the heavily favoured United States was a golden salve for the four-year-old wound.

Canadian Olympic women's hockey team members Thérèse Brisson (back left) of Dollard-des-Ormeaux, Québec, Cherie Piper, of Toronto, Ontario, and Becky Kellar (right) of Hagersville, Ontario, celebrate after receiving their gold medals. (CP PHOTO/Frank Gunn)

(Opposite – top) *Canadian players jump on top of their goalie Kim St-Pierre (33), of Chateauguay, Québec, as they celebrate their victory.* (AP Photo/Kevork Djansezian)

(Opposite – bottom) *Members of the Canadian Olympic women's hockey team pile on goaltender Kim St-Pierre.* (CP PHOTO/FrankGunn)

It was an amazing reversal. Four years ago, when women's hockey was an official medal sport for the first time, Canada won everything that season but lost the Olympics to the Americans. This time, the Americans entered the title tussle undefeated at 35-0, including eight wins over Canada.

"Anybody who ever doubted us, I don't think they doubt us anymore," said Geraldine Heaney, who announced her retirement following her 125th and final game for Canada. "There could not be a better way to end my career."

Caroline Ouellette, Hayley Wickenheiser and Jayna Hefford scored Canada's goals, and Kim St-Pierre was outstanding in goal, making 25 saves.

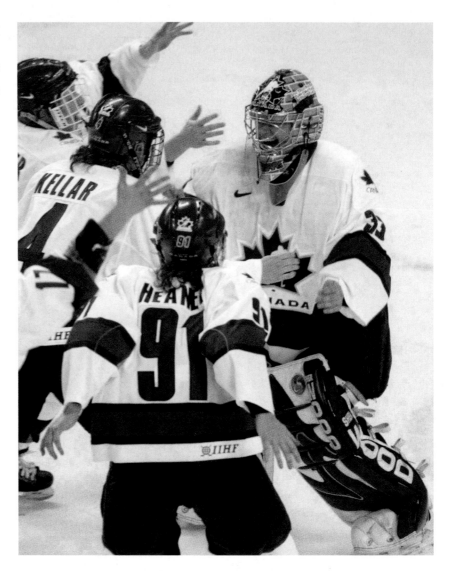

Canadian women's hockey team goalie Kim St-Pierre, of Chateauguay, Québec, is mobbed by teammates after the Canadian team won the gold medal.
(COA/Mike Ridewood)

Wickenheiser was named the tournament's most valuable player. She was holding her two-year-old son in one arm when she received her gold medal and bouquet of yellow roses.

"We've been waiting for this a long time, and it's real sweet," she said.

U.S. captain Cammi Granato was the first player on her team to receive a silver medal, and she wept, too. They had so wanted to retain the Olympic title in their homeland.

They had plenty of chances — 11 on power plays, which produced their two goals, by Karen Bye and Katie King. They had eight straight opportunities between the first and second periods. Canada got only four power plays from referee Stacey Livingston of Utica, New York.

"I've never seen anything like that," Wickenheiser said of the refereeing. "It was atrocious."

"They threw everything they had at us, and the referee wasn't on our side," said Heaney. "Kim played awesome."

Two members of Canada's women's hockey team show off their gold medals after the Canadian team won the gold medal game.
(COA/Mike Ridewood)

There were nearly as many Canadian flags and hockey jerseys in the crowd as American.

Wayne Gretzky brought his family, most of the players from the Canadian and U.S. men's teams cheered on their female counterparts, Jamie Salé made lots of noise with a cow bell sitting with figure skating partner David Pelletier, and singer Alanis Morissette was in the crowd of 8,500.

Ouellette's goal 1:45 into the game gave Canada an instant spark.

"They came out tentative and we could feel that," said Wickenheiser.

King tied it 1:59 into the second, and Wickenheiser restored Canada's lead at 4:10.

"We stayed calm," said Wickenheiser. "We could see the fear in their eyes."

Jayna Hefford's breakaway goal with one second remaining in the second was the winner.

"Our team had so much energy," said Jennifer Botterill. "Whoever was out there, we knew they were going to do a great job."

Bye's goal with 3:33 left made for a tight finish but coach Daniele Sauvageau's team wasn't about to let gold slip away.

"Looking down the line when all my teammates were getting their medals, that was the best part," said Botterill.

Atoning for the Nagano loss was paramount.

"I remember that feeling, and that's what motivated us," she said. "We were waiting for this moment for so long, and we felt ready."

There was no love lost between the teams.

The Canadians had heard stories of U.S. players throwing a Canadian flag on their dressing room floor.

Photos of Canadian players Lori Dupuis and Kelly Bechard in the athletes' village had American players' autographs scrawled across the faces.

Tears flowed down Sauvageau's cheeks, and those of many of her players, when "O Canada" was played.

(Opposite page)
Olympic gold medallists Canada's Danielle Goyette of St-Nazaire, Québec, Lori Dupuis, of Cornwall, Ontario, and Cassie Campbell, of Brampton, Ontario, left to right, sing along with the national anthem during medal ceremonies.
(CP PHOTO/Tom Hanson)

Canada's women's hockey team celebrate their gold medal win.
(CP PHOTO/ Tom Hanson)

"What stuck out at the last Olympics the most was being on the blueline and listening to their anthem," said forward Vicky Sunohara. "We did not want to hear that, we didn't want to hear it at all.

"We didn't. We heard ours."

Canada vs. U.S. Women's Gold Medal Game Summary

FIRST PERIOD	1. Canada, Ouellette 2 (Piper) 1:45
PENALTIES	Looney U.S. (holding) 6:17
	Kennedy U.S. (roughing) 10:54
	Botterill Cda (tripping) 12:15
	Wickenheiser Cda (delay of game) 14:05
	Brisson Cda (roughing) 17:01
	Sunohara Cda (cross-checking) 17:52
SECOND PERIOD	2. U.S., King 4 (Granato, Mounsey) 1:59 (pp)
	3. Canada, Wickenheiser 7 (Goyette) 4:10
	4. Canada, Hefford 3 (Kellar, Brisson) 19:59
PENALTIES	Kellar Cda (tripping) 1:11
	Oullette Cda (roughing) 4:51
	Chartrand Cda (tripping) 11:25
	Botterill Cda (tripping) 14:03
	Wendell U.S. (charging) 15:37
	Ouellette Cda (holding), Kennedy U.S. (roughing) 18:05
THIRD PERIOD	5. U.S., Bye 3 (Mounsey, Potter) 16:27 (pp)
PENALTIES	Wall U.S. (roughing) 0:44
	Kellar Cda (roughing) 1:49
	Sostorics Cda (body checking) 5:02
	Baker U.S. (holding stick), Dupuis Cda (high-sticking) 10:56
	Bechard Can (tripping) 16:04
SHOTS ON GOAL	Canada 9 10 10—29
	U.S. 11 9 7—27
GOAL	Canada: Kim St-Pierre (W,4-0)
	U.S.: Sara DeCosta, (L,2-1)
POWER-PLAYS *(goals-chances)*	Canada 0-4
	U.S. 2-11

Canadian Scoring for Tournament

	Goals	Assists	Points
Wickenheiser	7	3	10
Goyette	3	7	10
Hefford	3	4	7
Sunohara	4	2	6
Botterill	3	3	6
Ouellette	2	4	6
Piper	3	2	5
Brisson	2	3	5
Antal	2	1	3
Campbell	2	1	3
Chartrand	2	1	3
Dupuis	1	1	2
Shewchuk	1	1	2
Heaney	0	2	2
Sostorics	0	2	2
Bechard	0	1	1
Keller	0	1	1
St-Pierre	0	1	1

February 22, 2002

By B I L L   B E A C O N

WEST VALLEY CITY, Utah (CP) — A Canadian team that had a country wringing its hands early in the Olympic hockey tournament has made it to the gold medal game.

Steve Yzerman scored a goal and set up two more as Team Canada coasted to a 7-1 victory over lowly Belarus.

They will face the host United States for the gold medal on Sunday.

The Americans, a formidable offensive team, beat Russia 3-2 in the

Canadian Eric Lindros (88) of Toronto, Ontario, reaches for the puck shot by teammate Scott Niedermayer, not shown, as Belarus' goalie Andrei Mezin (31) looks on during the second period. Niedermayer was credited with the goal. (AP Photo/ Kevork Djansezian)

other semi-final of Friday, setting up a showdown between North American rivals on a wide-open Olympic-size rink.

"It means a lot to all of us — to the players and to Canadians back home," said Canadian captain Mario Lemieux. "It is something we haven't done in a long time.

"Winning a gold medal has been our goal since (a training camp) last August in Calgary. We are proud Canadians. Hockey is our sport. Everybody plays and watches it. For us to have a chance to do something special for our country is something we can all cherish for a long time if we win."

Canada is looking to win men's hockey gold for the first time since 1952 in Oslo, when it sent a senior team, the Edmonton Mercurys, to the Games.

Five surviving members of the Mercurys were among a large contingent of chanting, flag-waving Canadians in the less-than sellout crowd at the E-Center, which holds about 8,000 for the Games.

Several members of the Canadian women's team — who won gold on Thursday — were also in the crowd.

The TV audience back home for Sunday's men's game could be a record-breaker, judging from the women's final Thursday night. The Canadian women's win over the U.S. drew a peak audience of 6.225 million and averaged 4.54 million.

It pits a Canadian team that has used careful defensive play and opportunistic scoring against an American squad loaded with snipers like John LeClair, Brett Hull, Mike Modano and Tony Amonte.

And the United States has won hockey gold the last two times the Games were held on American soil — in 1960 in Squaw Valley, California, and 1980 in Lake Placid, New York.

The Canadian men finally broke through with a big offensive game against a weaker Belarus team that reached the semi-finals with a shock

Canada's goalie Martin Brodeur of Montreal, watches the puck bounce back out after a goal by Belarus' Ruslan Salei during the second period.
(AP Photo/Kevork Djansezian)

4-3 victory over Sweden on Wednesday.

"We tried to play the same way in this game," said Belarus defenceman Ruslan Salei, the team's only NHL player, who scored their only goal in the first period.

"But we made a couple of mistakes in the second period and that put the game away. Everyone (in Belarus) was outrageously happy when we beat Sweden. People were calling me and crying on the phone.

"We made history in Belarus that may never be repeated."

Canada's top line of Yzerman, Mario Lemieux and Paul Kariya was on the ice for all four goals as Canada built a 4-1 lead over the first two periods on goals from Yzerman, Kariya and defencemen Scott Niedermayer and Eric Brewer.

Simon Gagne, Eric Lindros, Jarome Iginla added confidence-building first goals in the third period for Canada, which will play its first Olympic final since 1994, when it lost to Sweden in a shootout in Lillehammer, Norway.

"It was important for us to get a good start and win by a large margin

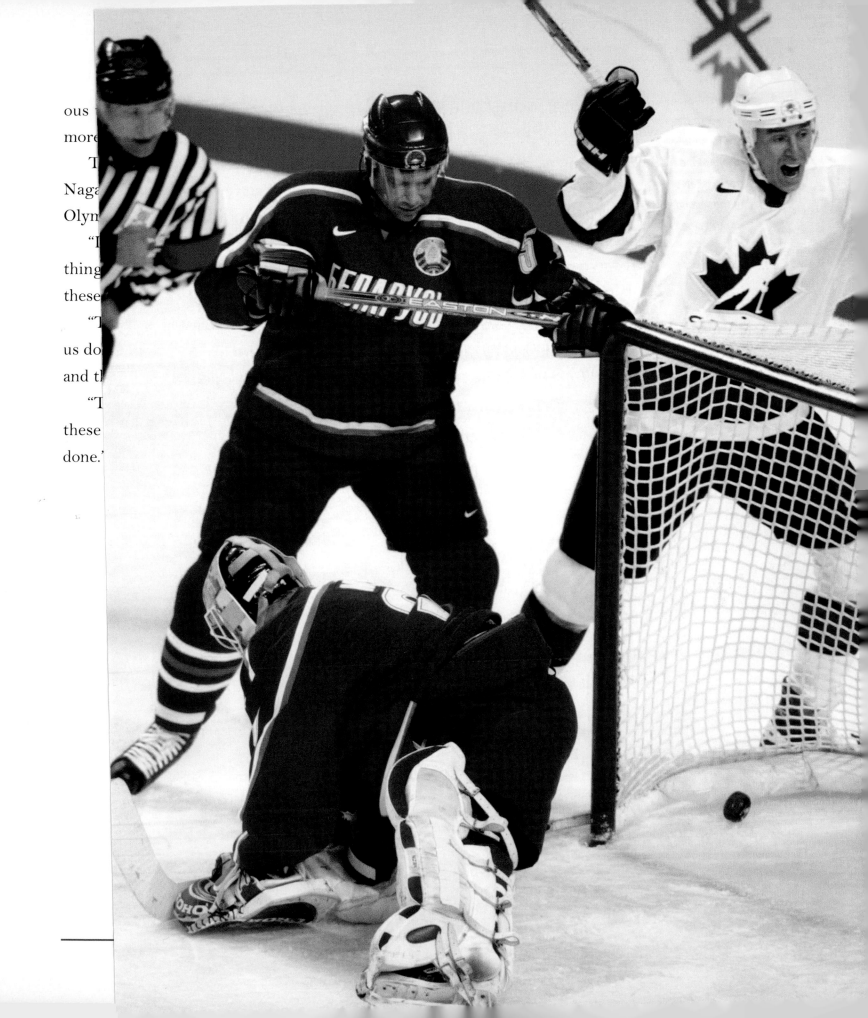

ous

more

T
Naga
Olyn

"I
thing
these

"T
us do
and tl

"T
these
done.'

Team Be...
Pankov s...
boards as Te...
Ed J...
Windsor, On...
past durin...
period. (COA...

Canada vs. Belarus Game Summary

FIRST PERIOD	1. Canada, Yzerman 2 (Sakic, Blake) 6:05
	2. Belarus, Salei 2 13:24
	3. Canada, Brewer 2 (Yzerman) 17:25
PENALTIES	Kopat Bel (high-sticking) 1:52
	Mikulchik Bel, Fleury Cda (roughing) 16:05
SECOND PERIOD	4. Canada, Niedermayer 1 (Lemieux, Kariya) 2:09 (pp)
	5. Canada, Kariya 2 (Yzerman, Lemieux) 13:28
PENALTIES	Kovalev Bel (holding) 1:10
	Jovanovski Cda (tripping) 2:38
	Peca Cda (cross-checking) 5:11
	Mikulchik Bel (boarding) 9:59
THIRD PERIOD	6. Canada, Gagne 1 (Peca) 5:21 (sh)
	7. Canada, Lindros 1 (Smyth, Nolan) 12:24 (pp)
	8. Canada, Iginla (Shanahan) 16:15
PENALTIES	Niedermayer Cda (high-sticking) 3:31
	Fleury Cda (hooking) 6:56
	Nolan Cda (roughing) 8:43
	Belarus bench (too many men; served by Makritsky) 10:52
	Tsyplakov Bel (roughing) 17:43
	Lindros Cda (slashing) 17:43
	Tsyplakov Bel, Lindros Cda (unsportmanlike conduct) 19:54
SHOTS ON GOAL	Belarus 3 6 5—14
	Canada 17 15 19—51
GOAL (shots-saves)	Belarus: Mezin (27-23), (L 1-4-0)
	Shabanov (24-21)
	Canada: Brodeur (W,3-0-1)
POWER-PLAYS (goals-chances)	Belarus: 0-5
	Canada: 2-3

Hockey game called Clash for Continental Gold

February 23, 2002

By ROBERT RUSSO

Salt Lake City (CP) – To Americans, it's a gold medal hockey game. For Canadians, it's a crusade.

American newspapers have dubbed Sunday's contest for Olympic gold as the Battle for the Border or the Clash for Continental Gold.

But there will be no national psychological meltdown in the United States should their squad have to settle for silver.

The dirtiest number in Canada right now is 1952 – the last time Canadian men's hockey players brought a gold medal back from the Olympics.

"This is pure hockey, pure Canada," said Skip Sullivan, a transplanted Torontonian now living in Salt Lake City.

"This is the real world championship, the real barometer of hockey supremacy and our national self-esteem depends on how well we measure up on that barometer."

Several Canadians old enough to remember 1972 and the see-saw Soviet-Canada Summit Series will tell you the context of Sunday's game is not the same.

There was more than hockey at stake 30 years ago. It was seen as a titanic tilt that pitted totalitarianism against democracy, black hats versus white hats, mysterious and coldly efficient Russian sportsmen against openly emotional Canadian warriors waging a battle beyond sports.

But Canadians do see an edge to this game against the Americans. The mouse wouldn't mind taking a bite out of the elephant next door.

"It's not like the Americans are the evil empire, but they're our biggest competitor culturally, they're the biggest economy and they barely know we exist," said Alaina Loukka.

Loukka is originally from Carston, Alberta, and now lives in Utah. Her husband is a native of Michigan. An invisible border is being drawn down the centre of their living room in front of the television.

"I brought my mom down from Alberta, so he feels outnumbered."

But he won't likely feel traumatized by an American loss. Canadians might. The reaction will also be seismic and generational if they win, according to defenceman Al MacInnis.

"Since I was young, all the kids playing on the street dreamed of winning Stanley Cups. But on Monday, they'll have another dream: winning a gold medal."

Americans have paid far more attention to Canada during the past fortnight than they normally would in a decade.

Canadian pairs skating darlings Jamie Salé and David Pelletier have been virtually adopted by Americans, who splashed them across the covers of *Time* and *Newsweek* after leading their northern neighbours in the outrage following the pairs competition.

The public grace displayed by Salé and Pelletier only seemed to reinforce America's view of their northern neighbour as a polite, if not benign, photo-negative of themselves.

There is little bitterness between players. In another week, Americans and Canadians will be inseparable, sitting in their NHL locker-rooms and yakking on their cellphones with their common agents.

How much bile can Brett Hull manufacture towards Canada? The transplanted American playing for the United States was born in Belleville, Ontario.

Canada's leaders include Steve Yzerman, an Ottawa native who became a U.S. citizen, and Mario Lemieux, owner of the Pittsburgh Penguins and employer of Herb Brooks, who just happens to coach the U.S. team.

Even Gretzky has lived in Los Angeles since 1988.

But Gretzky doesn't have to guess at what this game could mean to Canadians. In case he needed reminding, three television networks went live months ago just to cover his announcement of the Team Canada lineup.

He knows and fears the letdown Canada will suffer if it comes this close to winning, only to lose to the United States. Conversely, he is also keenly aware of the national elation that will be triggered by a Canadian victory.

"Nobody remembers who wins the silver," he said.

Canada ends 50 years of Olympic agony with gold medal at Games

February 24, 2002

By ROBERT RUSSO

WEST VALLEY CITY, Utah (CP) — The Olympic gold medal is returning to hockey's birthplace.

Team Canada soared from underachiever to Olympic champion Sunday, snuffing out a half-century of thwarted Olympic hockey ambitions and sending a hockey-nuts nation into delirium.

Canada's Ryan Smyth shows off his Olympic gold medal with Owen Nolan in the background.
(CP PHOTO/ Paul Chiasson)

The Canadian men thumped their American cousins 5-2, three days after the Canadian women won gold by defeating the U.S. 3-2.

Remarkably, Canada's gold came 50 years to the day after a collection of enthusiastic amateurs known as the Edmonton Mercurys won its last Olympic championship.

As the final minute dwindled down to its final seconds Sunday, both teams were serenaded with a leather-lunged version of "O Canada" from the thousands of Canadians who

(Opposite page) *Team Canada captain Mario Lemieux smiles as Theo Fleury skates holding the Canadian flag after they won over Team USA.* (COA/ Andre Forget)

(Previous page) *Canada's Theo Fleury waves a Canadian flag after winning the gold medal.* (CP PHOTO/Tom Hanson)

(This page) *Canada's goaltender Martin Brodeur is congratulated by Brett Hull of the USA.* (COA/Mike Ridewood)

some vigorous fist-pumping and a hug from his American wife, Janet.

"We desperately needed to win this tournament," a more subdued Gretzky said afterwards.

Canada's pursuit of the gold medal mesmerized Canadians. The CBC predicted the Sunday afternoon game would draw the largest TV audience in the nation's history — not just for sports, but for any event.

Canada staggered and stumbled into these Olympics. Tagged as the pre-tournament favourites, the world's best players looked pitiful in their first game against the Swedes and indifferent in a narrow win over the Germans.

Team Canada captain Mario Lemieux and goalie Martin Brodeur are surrounded by teammates as they pose for a team photo after they won the gold medal in hockey.
(COA/Andre Forget)

Canada's Mario Lemieux, Paul Kariya, Joe Sakic and Theo Fleury celebrate after beating the USA.
(Winnipeg Free Press/ Joe Bryksa)

A 3-3 tie with the Czech Republic was more promising.

Still Canadians fretted. Gretzky fumed.

The whole carefully constructed ensemble appeared to be coming unhinged after Gretzky accused the whole world of hating Canadians.

His basic message: When it comes to hockey, the world is a French figure skating judge.

It proved to be a brilliant stroke. He succeeded in shifting attention and criticism from his reeling charges onto his own aching back.

In case his message was lost, he called another news conference to reiterate what he'd said in the press conference the day before.

But with time to gel, a victory over Finland and then one brilliant stroke of good fortune — Swedish goalie Tommy Salo's inability to duck a puck fired at his cranium — Canada found itself catapulted into an easy semi-final draw against the plucky Belarusians who ousted Sweden, the class of the early going.

The Americans, who became the strongest and steadiest squad during the tournament, were forced to fend off a ferocious Russian team to reach the final.

There was the sense that this was a summit meeting of hockey talents in the current world. Americans, who make up about a quarter of all NHL players, were actually scoring slightly more goals-per-game than their Canadian counterparts before the pros took their Olympic break.

The requisite government representatives were on hand to lend the occasion the political heft needed to make it an event beyond sports.

U.S. Vice-President Dick Cheney, temporarily sprung from the secure undisclosed location that he's been squirrelled away in since September 11, represented the Bush administration.

Canada's own deputy prime minister, John Manley, made for cross-border political balance.

On wider rinks, with no fighting allowed and a premium placed on the

Canada's men's hockey team pose for a group photo with their Olympic gold medals. (CP PHOTO/Paul Chiasson)

artistic elements of the game — skating, shooting and passing — the game played during the Olympics bore only a slight resemblance to the duller NHL game.

But this contest was not without its savagery. These same players who, in a few days, will sit beside each other in NHL dressing rooms across the continent, proved adept at stickwork both legal and illegal.

American sniper Brett Hull appeared to be trying to undress Simon Gagné by running his stick up, down and under the Canadian forward's jersey.

But there was little of the rancour that would normally flow from a feisty game.

American players, silver medals adorning their sweaters, posed for pictures with Canadian players and their golds after the match.

There was also the realization that while Canada might have reclaimed its Olympic glory, it will be a battle to stay on top.

"I don't think you'll see any country ever dominate international hockey again," said Steve Yzerman, Canada's grey-bearded wizard. "We're all too balanced now for any team to dominate. I just hope they keep using NHL players in the Olympics."

Joe Sakic gets winning goal as Canada wins for first time in 50 years

February 24, 2002

By NEIL STEVENS

WEST VALLEY CITY, Utah (CP) — It will go down as one of the greatest hockey games ever played.

The Olympic men's final, won 5-2 by Canada, was hockey at its best.

One game for gold, and the all-star cast served up a treasured performance — with Joe Sakic getting to take the deepest bow.

From the start, the teams took different approaches.

The Americans used long passes through the neutral zone to try and spring shooters for the two-on-one breaks European teams favour, and Tony Amonte's goal to open the scoring proved the plan might work.

The Canadians stuck to a more traditional NHL style on offence. They had tried the long-pass strategy in their opener against Sweden and been burned 5-2. Coach Pat Quinn and his staff reminded their players during the second period of that game that riverboat gambling might not be the best approach.

Against the Americans, their strategy was to dump the puck deep into the U.S. zone instead of trying to stickhandle. They wanted to make the U.S. defencemen, many of them NHL senior citizens, expend as much energy as possible.

"We put a lot of pressure on them right from the start," said tournament MVP Joe Sakic. "We wanted to get (the puck) in deep.

"We knew they had a lot of turnover chances in the tournament and they capitalized on a lot of them so we wanted to make sure in the neutral zone and be smart and get (the puck) in and use our speed."

Canadian goalie Martin Brodeur blocks a shot as John LeClair (10) of the United States and Al Macinnis (2) of Canada slide into the net during the third period of the men's gold medal hockey game.
(AP Photo/ Kevork Djansezian)

Gretzky jumped out of his seat and threw his arms in the air and hugged those around him.

The Americans now had to throw caution to the wind.

"They started pressing late in the third and we were able to capitalize on a couple of chances," said defenceman Chris Pronger.

Sakic clinched it with a breakaway goal with less than two minutes remaining.

Gretzky jumped higher this time.

"We had a great game plan in place and played it to a T," said Pronger. "And Marty Brodeur made some great stops towards the end to preserve the victory."

Canada was due to win the Olympics. Sakic, Lemieux and their teammates would not be denied.

"We set out to do this and it wasn't easy," said defenceman Scott Niedermayer. "To be able to accomplish it is just amazing."

"It's unbelievable," said Pronger. "It's something you'll always be able to cherish, especially having it here in North America."

The tournament turnaround for Canada was its tie with the Czech Republic.

"We slowly built and kind of came in the back door and surprised a lot of people," said Pronger. "But we knew in that room what we could do."

The Americans gave it their best shot.

"We don't have anything to feel bad about," said defenceman Phil Housley. "It was a great experience for me and the rest of the guys.

"These memories are something I will carry with me for a long time."

Canada's Mario Lemieux (66), Paul Kariya (centre), Simon Gagne (21), Steve Yzerman (19) and Rob Blake (4) celebrate Canada's men's hockey team gold medal.

(COA/Mike Ridewood)

Canada vs. U.S. Men's Gold Medal Game Summary

FIRST PERIOD	1. U.S., Amonte 2 (Weight, Poti) 8:49
	2. Canada, Kariya 3 (Pronger, Lemieux) 14:50
	3. Canada, Iginla 2 (Sakic, Gagne) 18:33
PENALTIES	Niedermayer Cda (interference) 3:03
	Fleury Cda (cross-checking) 10:03
SECOND PERIOD	4. U.S., Rafalski 1 (Modano, Hull) 15:30 (pp)
	5. Canada, Sakic 3 (Jovanovski, Blake) 18:19 (pp)
PENALTIES	Hull U.S. (high-sticking) 9:27
	Miller U.S. (high-sticking) 10:19
	MacInnis Cda (interference) 14:40
	Roenick U.S. (tripping) 16:30
THIRD PERIOD	6. Canada, Iginla 3 (Yzerman, Sakic) 16:01
	7. Canada, Sakic 4 (Iginla) 18:40
PENALTY	Yzerman Cda (tripping) 13:43
SHOTS ON GOAL	Canada 11 17 11—39
	U.S. 10 14 9—33
GOAL	Canada: Brodeur (W,4-0-1)
	U.S.: Richter (L,2-1-1)
POWER-PLAYS (goals-chances)	Canada: 1—3
	U.S.: 1—4

Final Scoring Statistics – Canadian Men

	Goals	Assists	Points
Sakic	4	3	7
Lemieux	2	4	6
Yzerman	2	4	6
Iginla	3	1	4
Kariya	3	1	4
Gagne	1	3	4
Blake	1	2	3
Nolan	0	3	3
Jovanovski	0	3	3
Brewer	2	0	2
Niedermayer	1	1	2
Nieuwendyk	1	1	2
Fleury	0	2	2
Peca	0	2	2
Foote	1	0	1
Lindros	1	0	1
Pronger	0	1	1
Shanahan	0	1	1
Smyth	0	1	1

Canadian
fans erupt in
celebration after
gold medal
victory in
Olympic hockey

February 24, 2002

By JAMES McCARTEN
The Canadian Press

(Opposite) Hockey fans celebrate Team Canada win at the Salt Lake City Winter Olympics on Parliament Hill in Ottawa. (Ottawa Sun/Jason Ransom)

THEY TOOK TO THE STREETS with horns blaring, hearts bursting and Maple Leaf flags flying from hockey sticks Sunday after Canada's Olympic men's hockey team claimed its first gold medal in half a century.

Fans from coast to coast launched impromptu parades of unbridled patriotic joy after Canada beat the United States 5-2 in what many Canadians had come to consider their most important hockey game in 30 years.

"It's made us all foot-stomping, flag-waving Canadians, and we need to do that more often," said Bruce Thompson, who was celebrating in an

Hockey fans: (left to right) Shaun Fenniah, Mike Kuhnel, Daks Rees-Gower, Patrick Puff, Darren Oltmanns, Richie Sware, Dwayne Puff, and John Manning celebrate in Kuhnel's backyard ice rink in Edmonton. (Edmonton Sun/Darryl Dyck)

Canadian hockey fan Chin Wei Ho celebrates at a sports bar in downtown Montreal. (CP PHOTO/Ryan Remiorz)

Edmonton lounge along with hundreds of other fans.

"We haven't dominated anything in years, and today we dominated."

Early celebrations seemed peaceful.

In downtown Toronto, joyous fans streamed down bustling Yonge Street, many draped in flags and clad in Team Canada colours. Some leaned precariously out of car windows as they leaned on their car horns.

One fan was seen sprinting down the street, clad in nothing but a Canadian flag.

Alan Burnstein, a Detroit resident on a weekend trip to Toronto, was on Yonge Street when the crowds burst forth from the taverns and he suddenly found himself in the wrong place at the wrong time.

"If we had to lose, I'd like to lose to our neighbours to the north," said Burnstein. Nor was there cause for alarm, he added.

"I got a lot of ribbing the last couple of blocks but Canadians are friendly," he said. "If this were any other country I'd fear for my life."

In Brandon, Manitoba, they leaped to their feet and roared in the beer hall at the Scott Tournament of Hearts when the buzzer sounded.

And they stood again — the men removing their baseball caps — as Canada's anthem played and the jubilant faces of the Canadian men's hockey team appeared on two large television screens.

"It's the greatest thing I've ever seen in my life," said Sue Murray

Hockey fans (L-R) Brooke Dawkins, Andrea Keegan and Joanne Keegan celebrate team Canada's gold medal win at a downtown Ottawa bar. (CP PHOTO/ Jonathan Hayward)

from Flin Flon, Manitoba. "I'm a happy, happy person today. I cried. We all cried. Fifty years without a gold medal. We deserve it."

It didn't always look like it would go Canada's way.

There was palpable tension in taverns, shopping malls and living rooms across the country during the first two periods as the two teams looked evenly matched.

"There's no oxygen being consumed in here, because nobody's breathing any more," said Gail Rivett, one of dozens of fans at Toronto's Baton Rouge tavern who were glued to the TV screens.

Moments later, when Jarome Iginla put the Canadians ahead by two, the tension turned to celebration — fuelled largely by the fact that the win came at the hands of the American team.

"It's like the Maple Leafs versus the Montreal Canadiens thing, one of the outstanding rivalries in the history of sports," said Rivett, an executive with entertainment company Alliance Atlantis.

"It's not the end of the world, but it's something for a smaller country

Hockey fans celebrate at the intersection of Portage and Main in Winnipeg.
(Winnipeg Free Press/ Wayne Glowacki)

to rub in the face of a bigger one."

In Vancouver, fans were able to watch the game on a giant TV screen inside GM Place, the home of the NHL's Vancouver Canucks.

"That was better than losing my virginity!" screamed one fan in the frenzied moments after Canada won gold.

"I just knew that they would win," crowed 11-year-old Shaan Thind, bouncing up and down.

Bar patrons watching the game on a jumbo TV in Halifax screamed and stamped their feet in celebration and relief as the Iginla goal drained the wind from the American sails.

"It's fantastic," said university student Jonathan MacInnis.

In Calgary, some 500 people gathered at Canada Olympic Park, home to several events during the 1988 Winter Games, to cheer on Team Canada.

"This is a generational moment for all these people who didn't experience 1972," said John Mills, president of the Calgary Olympic Develop-

Crossing guard Tom Galarneau dresses in patriotic fashion in Halifax on Monday, February 25, 2002.
(HalifaxChronicle-Herald/Ted Pritchard)

ment Association.

"This is their moment and it will rival the Paul Henderson moment for years to come."

Prime Minister Jean Chretien issued a written statement that praised the Canadian team for their hard work and perseverance.

"The Maple Leaf is today flying proudly at the summit of the hockey world," said Chretien in congratulating both the men's and the women's squad, which claimed gold of its own by beating the U.S. on Thursday.

"In two golden weeks of triumph, the game that we have always called our own, that we have shared with the world, has become ours again."

Canadians are king in Kandahar

February 24, 2002

By STEPHEN THORNE

KANDAHAR, Afghanistan (CP) — The American army may have the men and machines but on this day in the desert the Canadians are king.

Their hockey team beat the United States 5-2 and Canadian soldiers in battle fatigues and hockey jerseys loved every second of it.

For once, they outnumbered their American brethren — by about 10 to one.

Corporal Bruce MacDonald of Dominion, Nova Scotia, (left to right) Corporal Allen Scott of Portugal Cove, Newfoundland, and Officer Brian Bodenmiller of the U.S. army's 306th Engineers out of Amityville, New York celebrate a goal by Team Canada against Team USA as they watch TV in Kandahar, Afganistan.
(CP PHOTO/Stephen Thorne)

They streamed in from the front lines, laid their rifles beneath their seats and for two and a half hours they cheered, they chanted and they jeered.

It was their moment in the sun, although in this dusty outpost, it was almost 3 a.m. Monday when Canada clinched its first Olympic hockey gold medal in 50 years.

"It was worth staying up for," said an elated Corporal Bruce MacDonald of the Forward Support Group out of Edmonton. "This was different, that's for sure."

Many troops didn't know until the last minute that Canada had even qualified for the gold medal game.

They made sure everybody knew the score this time.

Radiomen transmitted goals to their volunteer replacements out on the line — including some commanding officers — and, afterward, Canadian troops marched around the base, a former Taliban stronghold, hooting and hollering.

"We're celebrating a great victory," said Corporal Reg Keirstead of Miramichi, New Brunswick. "Two gold medals for Canada — men and women. That's the best."

"This is history," declared a young Corporal Dwaine Barker of Coachman's Cove, Newfoundland.

In Salt Lake City, the Canadians wore white and the Americans wore red. In Kandahar, they both wore camouflage — the Canadians green and the Americans tan.

Edmonton ice-maker snuck loonie into centre ice for Olympic luck

February 25, 2002

By **SUSAN HAGAN**

EDMONTON (CP) — Trent Evans returned from the Winter Olympics a dollar short, but proud that he embedded a lucky loonie at centre ice at the E-Center in Salt Lake City. Both the Canadian women's and men's hockey teams successfully skated to gold over top of that loonie.

"If that had anything to do with the good luck of both teams winning the gold, I think that's awesome," the Edmonton-based icemaker said Monday. "I'll cherish that forever."

When Wayne Gretzky, executive director for the men's team, held up the bronze-plated loonie at a post-win news conference Sunday, Evans was off to the side beaming with pride.

BRUCE MACKINNON

But sneaking the dollar coin into the ice and keeping it secret from his 13 American ice maintenance counterparts proved to be nerve-racking.

Evans cooked up the plot February 4 when he noticed the Olympic logo that surrounded centre ice didn't have a dot to mark the middle. That's when he decided to improvise.

"But I only had a dime," said Evans, who was one of three Canadians hired to tend the ice. He is supervisor of event operations at Edmonton's Skyreach Centre – home of the Edmonton Oilers and known throughout the National Hockey League as having some of the best ice in North America.

Evans returned the next day and placed the loonie over top of the dime, instantly creating a myth, and, some would argue, a whole lot of luck. "So there was really $1.10 at centre ice. They were both Canadian coins and, sure enough, the loonie turned out to be excellent luck."

Though the colour of the coin blended nicely with the Olympic logo, if players squinted closely, they would have been able to make out the markings of the loonie.

By the third day of the Games, Evans became nervous about being found out, so he and a colleague camouflaged the spot with yellow paint.

But keeping the secret proved to be more difficult than concealing the coin.

"I told too many people," he said.

Evans brought three women on the hockey team into the fold in hopes of keeping their spirits up. But when they celebrated after the gold, he thought the gig was up.

"I was concerned when the girls started kissing centre ice because at any time it wouldn't have been hard to pull out the loonie like I did (Sunday)," he said. "It took me 10 seconds."

However, the coin stayed embedded through it all.

After the men's gold medals were presented, Evans slunk through the dressing room and onto the ice to retrieve his charm.

Though he had a moment in the spotlight, a good feeling about his lucky charm, and the thrill of handing Gretzky his good-luck coin, there may be consequences.

"It's a huge story (in the U.S.)," he said. "I can't see myself working another international tournament for what happened."

But was his moment in the spotlight worth the secrets, the worry, and the sacrifices?

"Oh, definitely," he said. "I'm Canadian wholeheartedly."

The loonie will go on display at the Hockey Hall of Fame in Toronto to commemorate Canada's two gold hockey medals at the 2002 Winter Games. It was the first gold for the men in 50 years and sweet retribution for the women who lost in the gold-medal match four years ago.

Though Evans doesn't have the coin as a memento, he didn't exactly go home empty-handed.

"I've still got the dime," he said.

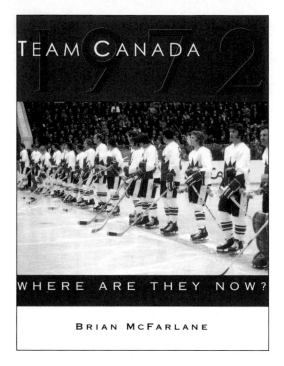